GW00854817

Bangkok in 3 Days

The Definitive Tourist Guide Book That Helps You Travel Smart and Save Time

Finest City Guides

This certainly isn't the only travel guide for travelers to Bangkok, but it's the only one to provide you with all you need to know if you only have a few days to spend there. You'll want to be more organized if you have only a little time to spend in this exciting city.

This guide offers you valuable information about the most important highlights in Bangkok. We include historical monuments, places with high architectural or artistic value, and social attractions. Many of these places are already landmarks, but this guide aims at helping you organize your trip by including only what are really must-see attractions.

We offer you lots of useful tips on where to go in Bangkok if you're interested in the culture of the city, in its art galleries, theaters and concert venues. We'll also include helpful information for people of all ages. This book gives you the information you'll need to plan and execute your trip, from the currency used in Thailand and how to get around, to tipping habits in-country.

Bangkok offers a truly memorable experience to anyone who knows how to travel intelligently and save time and unwanted expenses. Enjoy it and make the best of your visit!

Here is a preview of what you will learn in this guide:

- What makes Bangkok attractive to tourists
- Key information about the capital of Thailand
- How to get there
- Tips for getting around in the city
- Advice on accommodations
- Recommended tourist attractions that are a must-see, even if you stay only three days
- Tips on what and where to eat/drink if you want to experience typical flavors or interesting places in the capital
- What you should see if you're interested in culture and entertainment
- Recommendations for specific events during your stay

Table of Contents

1. Introduction

Some travel guides give you literally too much information to process. If you're only spending a few days in Bangkok, you don't need to know ALL the little tucked-away places that you might visit if you had a week or so to spend there. At the same time, you need solid information on the most important and entertaining sites, or you'll be wandering around and never accomplish anything in three days.

We give you plenty of information to allow you to dive into the culture of Thailand, and witness its historic sites, while still allowing time to enjoy the best Thai cuisine and enjoy the comforts of the best luxury hotels, if those are your choice. (You'll also have information on the cheaper places to crash, in case you'd rather spend your money on seeing the sights rather than sleeping in luxury.)

Bangkok is a mixture of earthiness and mysticism, and this is played out in the daily life of the busy city. Mixing old historic gems with modern buildings, the city has something for everyone to enjoy. It's also known as the city of the god Indra, the residence of Emerald Buddha and the city of angels.

From the opulent to the simple, there are plenty of things to tempt you in Bangkok. Read on and learn what you need to know when visiting the Thai capital for just a few days.

2. Key Information about Bangkok

Money Matters

Thailand's currency is called "Baht". The majority of vendors in the city prefer cash for most transactions, although the larger hotels and shops also accept credit cards. 100 Baht is about $3 USD, and in Thai currency, worth 100 Satang. Thailand can be enjoyed and appreciated for very little in USD. The currency you'll use most includes 1, 2, 5 and 10 Baht, in bills and coins.

It's easier to exchange your money when you arrive than it is to use a Visa or Master Card for local purchases, particularly for Americans. Many credit card companies charge 2-5% fees for any international transactions. Some shops accept credit cards, but the local vendors may also charge you more for using them. This is especially true of smaller shops, since the merchants are charged for each transaction.

Major restaurants and hotels and larger stores won't charge extra if you want to use your credit card. In addition, you can use ATMs to get cash, but the credit card companies usually charge high fees for that, as well. Thai banks may even charge you 150 Baht or more if you use a foreign card to get cash from ATMs.

Tipping

In Thailand, tipping is not a rule. It's entirely up to you if you want to leave a small expression of gratitude. Nobody will expect or silently demand a tip in Bangkok. Most restaurants and hotels include a 10% charge on the bill, so it's about equal to the tip you'd have left anyway.

In case you want to be generous and you totally enjoyed the service, you can leave 30-50 Baht for the porter or waiter. Loose change is fine to leave behind. In more expensive and stylish restaurants, you can leave 10-15% of what you ordered to show your appreciation. Nobody will refuse, but they won't expect it, either.

Cultural Norms and Etiquette

Although you can keep your individual personality and fashion when you visit Bangkok, it's always good to be aware of a few norms, if you want people not to be surprised or worried about your behavior. Politeness is highly valued in Thailand and you are expected to behave in a friendly and calm manner in all social situations.

Expressions of anger are not welcome. The overall atmosphere of Thailand is one of easygoingness and enjoyment of the world. In such a context, one might think Thai locals are very accepting of everything. This is likely to be the case in more private spheres of life. When it comes to public behavior, people of Thailand are rather traditional, polite, and well mannered.

As such, they might expect others (even short-term tourists) to show a form of respect for their own conventions and values. For instance, the image of the King and dressing in ways that cover much of your body are very important in Thailand. Not only in temples should you not wear revealing clothing, but also when you go out in public places.

Of course, nobody will "punish" you for having your own personality, but you should be aware of what locals usually do and appreciate. You do not want to feel estranged when visiting Bangkok.

3. Transport to and in Bangkok

Most people travel to Thailand by plane. Bangkok is a busy transport hub that almost every large (even low-cost) airline will reach. Please remember that, if you come from a Western country, your flight might take over 10 hours. However, flying to Bangkok remains the most comfortable option. You can also take the train from Malaysia and Singapore, depending on your route and your starting point.

Are there reasonably priced flights to Bangkok? Since we're talking about a country that is situated on the Asian continent, you must realize that, if you're coming from the States or Europe, a few hundred euros or dollars is a good enough price when you want to visit Thailand. Chinese Airlines offers a flight from and to the US at price of approximately 500 USD.

As for European connections, Emirates airline is likely the best provider. Etihad is another company based in the United Arab Emirates that is well known for connecting major European cities to Thailand. The Thai national airline, Thai Airways, is also a good idea you might want to consider. The low cost option if you want to fly inside Thailand is Bangkok Airways or Air Asia, which can take you to several destinations quickly if you want to stay longer in Thailand and visit more places.

Getting around in Bangkok reflects the same mixture of modern technology and antique-looking charm. Why? On one hand, you have the "regular" subway transport you can find in every major world capital. The Skytrain (BTS) adds to a fast and efficient public transportation network. They connect the major points in the city.

You can also get around by river taxis and express boats to explore other areas. Such transport is cheap enough in Thailand. The rather traditional and appreciated means of transport, the tuk-tuk, is another way of moving around. This is a three-wheeled motorcycle attached to a passenger carriage that many tourists love traveling by.

However, nowadays it retains an air of entertainment transportation rather than being the major means people use when they are really in a hurry and want to do things. Try it anyway!

If you like exotic ideas, you can also choose a trip by songthaew, a sort of truck with benches on either side that fits the Thai version of a minibus. Alternatively, you can go by the (boring) bus and see the city in its entire splendor as in any other capital or town.

In case you wonder if transport is expensive, the answer is not at all. You can buy a BTS pass if you are truly on a budget and you want to save some more. The so-called Rabbit card will help you access all stations. Fees increase by stop in Thailand. For this reason, it's better to purchase a one-day ticket that will let you stop wherever you want and travel throughout the city. The price for one day is 120 Baht, which is quite low, especially when you come from a country in Western Europe, North America or Australia.

If you prefer a universal means of transport that can make you feel comfortable and casual and allow you to move as you wish, you can rent a car. There are many companies in Bangkok which offer you the possibility to rent a car starting from 20-22 USD/day, which you will probably find affordable enough.

4. Accommodations

Accommodations are on the cheap side in the Thai capital. Regardless of your actual budget, you are likely to find your stay in Bangkok quite affordable and pleasant (for this reason and for others). However, in case you are a student, and are looking for cheaper rates, or you come from a country where income is not very high, you can always consider budget accommodations in Bangkok. What does this mean exactly?

The lowest price you are likely to find is somewhere around 10-15 USD/night. Your good options are Amarin Inn (close to the old city), Thanapa Mansion (near the airport), The Urban Age Hostel, Place Inn Hotel, etc. You are welcome to try these places if you wouldn't mind saving some money by using cheaper accommodations.

If you want a nice place in a great area while not breaking the budget, go for a standard hotel that many tourists from all over the world can afford. What is recommended? You have a myriad of places to choose from: 48 Ville (near the airport), Bhiman Inn, Khaosan Holiday, Mango Lagoon

Place, Suneta Hostel, Chaosan, Lucky House etc. (all in the old city – Chao San), FAB Hostel Bangkok, Baan Bovorn (in Sathorn area), Cooper, Lullaby Inn Silom, Take a Nap Hotel, 13 Coins Antique Villa (in Silom), Ibrik Resort by the River, Woodlands Inn Hotel (on the marvelous riverside), etc.

How much does renting a room cost in such places? Even in a few standard hotels, you are likely to find something for 10-20 USD, if you mainly just want a room to sleep in. In case you are looking for extra facilities and higher comfort, prices will range from 20 USD to 40 USD per night. In more special locations, they can also go higher. However, you have a very wide array to choose from when it comes to finding "regular" accommodations in the capital of Thailand.

4-star hotels range from 25-60 USD per night, also depending on their location and how far from the city center or key tourist spots they are. You can even get 4-star accommodations for less than 15-20 USD if you care mostly about price. Consider Loft 77, Crystal Suites, City Point Hotel, Aphrodite Inn, Centric Place, Diamond House, Dynasty Grande, Forum Park Hotel, Orchid Resort, etc.

Other 4-star accommodations will cost you in a price range of 50-100 USD. However, if you're lucky and not lofty, you can even get away with 35-60 USD/night. Pick one on this list or others that you can find in your area of choice: Jasmine City Hotel, Cinnamon Residence, Bangkok Patio, Arun Residence, Grand China Hotel, Indra Regent, Marvel Hotel Bangkok, Rembrandt Hotel, Olive Residence, etc.

If you don't care about budget at all, then don't hesitate - book pure luxury in a 5-star hotel. Prices are again flexible and generous. You can pay around 100 USD or more per night (as in other world capitals), but you can also benefit from the low Thai prices and find something in the range of 60-100 USD/night. A few worthwhile examples are Amari Watergate Bangkok, Praya Palazzo, Sofitel So Bangkok, Montien Riverside Hotel, Hotel Muse Bangkok, etc. Find the most fitting option and enjoy your stay!

5. Sightseeing

Bangkok might look like a rare (and maybe unpolished) diamond for many tourists. It has a charming blend of simplicity and opulence, depending on what you want to see and where you go. In any case, this overall impression strikes many tourists who visit the Thai capital and even return there on future trips.

Inexpensive markets sit side by side with enigmatic and solemn Buddhist temples, a fascinating paradox that has lured many people to the city. So what should you consider when you visit Bangkok? Let's take it step by step.

The Grand Palace and Wat Prakaew

In the old city there's a captivating center of art and spirituality (which often go hand in hand in Thailand). By far one of the major attractions of Bangkok, the Grand Palace was built in the 18th century and it was for about 150 years the residence of Thai royals. Nowadays this complex of buildings is treasured mainly for its architectural and spiritual value. Symbolic for Thai art, the splendid Grand Palace impresses with its combination of finesse and intricate architectural elements.

While the royal family doesn't live there anymore, this palace still maintains the air of a "residence of kings", at least through its spiritual component that leaves the impression of being "outside the reach of mortals". There's something that defies the mundane and the ephemeral when you see the Grand Palace.

Within the Palace complex you will also find the famous Wat Prakaew, the Temple of the Emerald Buddha. This mixture of opulent, sophisticated art, high social class (royalty) and religious content is the distinguishing mark of this important Bangkok center. The small, but highly precious Emerald Buddha dates from the 15th century and makes Bangkok the heart of this spiritual path.

Many people come to Thailand to get familiar with Buddhist teachings "right from the source". The statue is involved in important celebrations and rituals performed by the King of Thailand. The Palace is still used nowadays for receptions and coronations and this creates the impression of continuity in the line of royal participation.
Keep in mind that visiting this place will require conforming to a specific dress code (e.g. long garments, shirts and blouses with sleeves, no

bare feet in sandals, etc.). The key is being well covered as a sign of reverence to Buddha and the royal atmosphere in this center.

However, you won't be sent away if you come dressed in very revealing or casual clothes. They will only ask for a deposit to offer you more modest clothes that you'll be able to put on in a booth near the entrance. The fee for visiting the whole complex of buildings amounts to about 500 Baht.

The Temple of Dawn (Wat Arun)

This temple is another emblem of Thailand. Located on the West bank of the Chao Phraya River, its design shows Gothic elements rather than the traditional architecture of Thailand, with its golden shrine and majestic opulence. No less impressive, this temple reigns on the riverside and is made of colorfully decorated spires and ensembles of stairs that strike the viewer as fascinating and compelling. Entry to this temple is around 100 Baht. You can take a boat for a minimal fee to get to it. This temple was built in the 18th century and it was the initial home of the Emerald Buddha.

Floating Markets

Tourists usually find these markets irresistible. While they are not an architectural or cultural treasure of Thailand, one cannot ignore the fact that such a thing qualifies as one of the top attractions of Bangkok. They are usually geared towards tourists. In addition, they are quite affordable. What can you see when you visit such a market? Usually they are set up in boats full of products, floating on water. You can taste and purchase many tropical fruit types and vegetables and even enjoy coconut juice on the spot! Even cooked food is available – what more could you ask for?

Hardly equaled by anything else in the world, Thai floating markets are a bona fide symbol of this culture. If you want to explore things comprehensively, you can enjoy a guided tour of Damnoen Saduak market. Other markets are Taling Chan Market, Tha Kha, Amphawa, or Bang Wiang markets.

Chinatown

This part of Bangkok lures tourists with Chinese temples and street food, which are a rather practical and appropriate combination! You can also visit it for its gold shops and market stalls. Wat Traimit is a wonderful temple, famous for being home to the largest golden Buddha in the world. It receives visitors from all over the world who come to Chinatown either to enjoy it as a museum, or as a form of pilgrimage.

The Chinagate is already a symbol of Chinese spirituality and culture and it marks the largest "Chinatown" in the world, in Bangkok. In the same area, you can see the Wat Mangkol Kamalawat, the largest Buddhist temple in the Thai capital. It contains not only Buddhist, but also Confucian and Taoist shrines.

Wat Pho

A hub of meditation, Thai massage, and other spiritual and wellbeing activities, Wat Pho is also known by the name of the Temple of the Reclining Buddha. It hosts the huge statue that is 46 meters long and covered in gold leaf. Most tourists come here to see the statue and enjoy various activities that are related to Buddhist spirituality.

Wat Pho is also the center of the most important school of Thai massage. You might want to leave this attraction for your last day in Bangkok, when you can relax more and "breathe out" all the tiredness and hustle of your previous days. You can visit the whole temple for about 100 Baht and you can also go for an option that includes an English-speaking guide for 300-400 Baht. This might be worth it for the intricate murals that you are likely to want to find out more about.

Wat Pho was the first public university in Thailand. It specialized in religion, science, and literature. Nowadays people visit this center either to learn, or to benefit from Thai massage. This massage is a special type – unlike others, it invigorates you and it includes yoga techniques for a more extensive effect on the body and mind.

Chao Phraya and the Bangkok Canals

The riverside is one of the most sought after spots in the Thai capital. Picture a sort of Asian Venice! While it doesn't have the antique and artistic charm of the Italian town on water, the Bangkok riverside still attracts many tourists for its splendid view and taxi boat trips.

Exploring the riverside doesn't take too much money and you'll surely enjoy calmly moving on the water as you go by boats of locals who have their own businesses. Beautiful houses and people are quite a sight to behold from a great vantage point as you take a boat trip on Bangkok canals.

Jim Thompson House

This house is the work of Jim Thompson, an American who loved Thai culture. It is surrounded by a gorgeous garden and is located on the bank of the Saen Saeb canal. This complex consists of six traditional Thai teakwood houses.

Jim Thompson was an architect who also collected Asian art. Among his life passions, there was also the splendid Thai silk, which he introduced to major fashion houses in the world after he settled in Thailand in the 1950s. The house he left behind is an authentic museum that is worth visiting as one of the most interesting and unique Thai attractions.

Lumphini Park

This park is the largest in Thailand and a great place for relaxation and entertainment in Bangkok. Even if you are in a hurry, you should visit it for its beautiful public spaces, artificial lake, and vegetation. It was created in the 3rd decade of the last century on the property of King Rama VI. It is famous for the King's majestic statue, bird watching, an interesting library and Buddhist Dharma activities.

The Vimamnek Mansion

This important museum is solid proof that Bangkok is not only about spiritually-oriented culture and art. This building was once a royal residence and dates from the end of the 19th century. Apart from many collections and items that belonged to King Rama V, this museum now hosts many art works that are representative of Thai culture, in general. It is also the world largest teakwood mansion.

Bangkok National Museum

This museum is the largest in Southeast Asia. Here you can learn about Thai history and art in a rather "classical" way, which cannot be experienced in any other world capital. However, in the middle of so much Thai exoticism, it is certainly worth having a comprehensive view of the Thai culture. This museum dates from the 19th century and it displays collections and facts about many periods in Thai history as well as Buddhist art.

6. Eat & Drink

If you visit Thailand, you are likely to want to taste traditional Thai food. Although there are many places with good food from all over the world (e.g. US barbeque, French cuisine, etc.), if you stay in the Thai capital for several days, it's recommended that you try the incredibly delicious Thai food. Where should you go?

First of all, beware of the many street vendors who "prey" on tourists, and may offer anything, assuring you that it is a true Thai dish. There are some very good ones but many that don't compare to the real thing.

Locals are prone to being more fussy and critical about Thai food, so here are a few restaurants that are considered awesome by everyone (locals included).

La Table de Tee is for gourmet eaters. You will get five dishes (including two small ones between your main food items) if you go for dinner, which is advisable. The overall price is about 1000 Baht, but with everything you get, it's worth it: food quality, atmosphere, design, food presentation and service. This place is perfect if you want to celebrate something in a larger group or you simply want to enjoy top quality Thai cuisine.

More casual eating is what you can easily get from street vendors, provided that you go to the right places. Chinatown is one of the best options. Here the quality of the street food is exceptional and you can find an amazing variety that can please even the most easily bored or experienced tourists.

In Yawovarat, food will also appeal to you through all your senses: you can actually smell it on the street! This area is most lively in the evening. The bonus is that you can try "sample food" in small portions. Make sure you don't go overboard and fill up with just samples! This place is a treasure for the many types of curry you can find and enjoy here.

Street food is quite cheap and tasty in Thailand. You will be totally sated with a meal that costs only about 150-200 Baht. Try an egg noodle soup or the Pad Thai for a great traditional experience.

Kalpapruek is located on the 7th floor of the Central World shopping destination. Here you can have a nice meal, as you take a relaxing break from shopping. This place is reasonably priced and it can offer you not only Thai, but also world cuisine. However, for a Thai experience try the Red Chicken Curry, the delicious cakes, the many savory types of smoothies, or the chicken with cashew nuts. These foods are among the things that make this restaurant famous.

If you want to try a bona fide Papaya Salad (you've probably had various versions in other parts of the world), a great place for this is Somtum Der. This restaurant is on the small side and its atmosphere is cozy and intimate. However, the Som Tam is hard to top! Not only are they masters at this dish, but also they've turned it into their personal specialty and pride. They prepare about eight versions of Som Tam. You can also have tasty desserts here for a great price, too. This place is casual, but the food it offers is very authentic.

What if you love noodle soup? The best place for this is probably Bamee Sawang, a noodle café that attracts both locals and tourists. They have a personalized noodle soup recipe which was inherited as a family tradition. If you also want to experiment with another simple, yet typically Thai dish, namely the Pad Thai, you can grab it at Thip Shamai. You don't have to expect anything fancy when you come here: a quick stop on your way to exploring Bangkok is great. The food is authentic and you can enjoy it with a tasty orange juice that also makes this small place quite well known.

Where can you get something to drink and have fun in Bangkok? When you just want to go out and enjoy a nice evening, choose Thonglor, one of the coolest areas in Bangkok. Here you can find an amazing place, Studio Lam, where you can drink homemade herbal Thai liquor and listen to quality music. The emphasis here is on both drinks and atmosphere.

J. Borosky Mixology is the right place if you want a real taste of Bangkok nightlife. This place is great for more "underground" fun and amazing cocktails. If you prefer a fancier place, try WTF (Wonderful Thai Friendship). Contrary to the first impression, this place is very welcoming. Apart from the myriad of high quality cocktails, they serve typically Thai snacks and they have a nice art gallery to please their visitors.

7. Culture and Entertainment

The Bangkok Art and Culture Centre is a huge building with 11 floors. The top three are exhibition halls. This center is amazing for modern art lovers who want to see more than sculpture and painting. Here you can find video productions, photography, installation and performance art. Make sure to visit it when you do have some free time at hand! In this center, Western ideas and Thai tradition blend and the academic goes hand in hand with avant-garde artistic productions. Entrance is free, so everyone is welcome!

The Bangkok Sculpture Center is another significant cultural venue for people who want to tap deeply into Thai art. This building focuses on modern Thai sculpture and houses over 100 works by different artists.

Patravadi Theater and Studio 9 is a unique venue that you shouldn't miss. An important figure of Thai theater turned her compound into an open-air theater in 1992. Now you can find a café, a gallery, and a theater in the same place, and enjoy modern and engaging productions. Apart from art shows, you can also attend classes, if you have enough time. Studio 9 is a newer addition to this venue, where you can also listen to live music.

Queen's Gallery is an interesting place that tourists and art lovers with refined taste will adore. It was dedicated to Queen Sirikit and it displays top-notch internationally appreciated art. It has several floors and, apart from art galleries, you will find a wonderful gift shop with rare items.

Aksra Theater is a major Thai venue where you can enjoy both modern and traditional performances. Prices are affordable and the theater building is also interesting. Its style is majestic and opulent and it perfectly evokes a combination of Western comfort and Asian art. The special feature of this theatre is a permanent troupe of hun lakorn lek puppetry.

The Thai Puppet Theater is another intriguing venue that might offer you the perfect glimpse into Thai art and culture. The same hun lakhon lek puppets are used for performances here and handled by three dancing "actors".

If you prefer a comfortable and modern place where you can enjoy music performances rather than "high culture", you can go to the Diplomat Bar. This place is an exquisite jazz lounge with enthralling flower installations and a mysterious atmosphere. Another option is AdHere 13th; a more casual place for music jams where you can have a lot of fun on any night of the week.

Brick Bar has Western overtones, but this makes it even more intriguing. Go there if you are a fan of blues and jazz. This music club is one of the fanciest in Bangkok and for this reason, you can often find lots of amazing clients here.

Impact is a large place where most big pop-rock concerts take place. Discover in advance if there's something you might want to check out, as you will have to purchase your ticket quite early.

8. Special Events in Bangkok

The Bangkok Fringe Festival takes place in January and February and it includes music, dance, and theater performances. Its main location is the great Patravadi Theater. During this festival Eastern and Western concepts and productions come alive in the same place to enchant the public. However, the weekend evening shows are performed in the native language of Thailand, so it might be difficult to make the best of them.

Chinese New Year is an interesting celebration that you should check out if you visit Thailand in January. Chinatown becomes a hub for dance, fireworks, and Chinese symbols. Food is even more abundant and tasty than in other periods of the year and you can even enjoy Chinese opera during this festival.

Songkran takes place in April and it is dedicated to purification and regeneration through water. While some Thai people turn it into a rather funny feast of water throwing, originally this celebration was meant to be a ritualistic purging. There are special shows during this celebration (where most Bangkok locals gather) as well as ceremonies in Buddhist temples.

Visakha Bucha is likely the holiest day in Thailand. It celebrates the birth, death, and enlightenment of Buddha. Devotees bring food and gifts to Buddhist monks in temples and there are interesting ceremonies as everyone surrounds the temples in the candlelight. This event takes place every year in May or June. During this day, people are not allowed to drink alcohol.

The Queen's Birthday on the 12th of August marks a more extensive celebration. It is also Mother's Day. People celebrate in the street with shrines, candlelight, and illuminations. The atmosphere is great and there are no restrictions for visitors who wish to take part in the ceremonies of the day.

If you visit Bangkok in September and October, you'll be able to enjoy the International Festival of Music and Dance. It is a major cultural event in Thailand that organizes opera, ballet, dance, jazz and classical music performances.

The Bangkok International Film Festival takes place in September. While you are probably not going to spend your time in the cinema as a tourist, you will probably like watching one or two films during the 10-day festival that gathers many genres and countries.

The Vegetarian Festival is a ten-day celebration of a meat-free world. Its origin and tradition are Chinese. For this reason, Chinatown fills with veggie food and people who are there to taste it. You can also listen to Chinese opera around shrines on the streets of Bangkok if you happen to visit the city in October.

The Golden Mount Temple Fair is the biggest event of its kind. The streets are full of passersby who want to look or purchase things. It is located around Long Kratong and it can certainly be a great experience for a tourist. Enjoy it if you visit Bangkok in November!

The King's Birthday on the 5th of December is an important celebration that also takes the form of the so-called Father's Day. People gather on the streets of Bangkok to show respect to the King on this national holiday. The King greets the crowd by means of a speech in the Royal Plaza. Dance, fireworks, traditional music, candles, and decorations bring the city to full life on this day that is definitely one of the most interesting and animated in the whole year.

9. Safety in Bangkok

Bangkok is not inherently more dangerous than any other city its size. That said, you need to always be aware of your surroundings. The crimes perpetrated on tourists are mainly those like pickpocketing, credit card scams and offers to sell fake gemstones or other goods. The most common pickpocket areas are the main railway station and the Chatuchak weekend market north of Bangkok.

When you use credit cards, keep them in view. Don't let waiters, etc. take them away to ring up your bill. Check all your bills twice, to ensure that they are accurate.

Gems are involved in the most common Bangkok scams. People may approach you outside major tourist attractions and tell you that the attraction is not open. They will be friendly and suggest another place to visit, and that the government is sponsoring a gem sale there, one that is only held once a year.

These "helpful" thieves will offer you a ride in an open air taxi to the so-called "special" temple.

Once there, another helpful stranger will speak to you and "mention" the gem sale. If you agree to go to the shop, you will be coerced into buying real gemstones, which of course theirs are not. If you buy and have them appraised when you get home, you will find out that they actually have only a minimal value.

10. Conclusion

This guide has been designed to provide you with the necessary information and recommendations to turn your stay in Bangkok into a fruitful and memorable trip. Bangkok is a place that might seem too far-off or "low profile" at first impression, especially after you've visited many places that are also tech and high culture hubs where world development is set in motion.

However, this couldn't be farther from the truth. Bangkok is a gem in its own way: a center of ancient spirituality that is still flourishing and developing today, the Thai capital can convince anyone that along with high artistic productions and creation, there are also more simple kinds of values and interesting things to enjoy.

As a celebration of earthly simplicity and minimalism accompanied by opulent architecture where Buddhist traditions flourish and enchant visitors, Bangkok is a remarkable sight to experience and remember. Many tourists return there either to enjoy the quiet and natural life close to water and in the middle of exotic nature, or to indulge in the benefits of yoga, meditation, and Thai massage.

As a travel guide meant to show you what you can include in three days, this book aimed at combining entertainment value and cultural treasures, which will satisfy many people who visit this alluring capital. Apart from many practical tips that can help you find your way through a culture you are probably not very familiar with, this guide provided you with numerous tips on how to take advantage of more "mundane" joys when visiting Thailand.

Quality traditional food, amazing festivals, and other forms of entertainment can make your trip to Bangkok a memorable one. The next step is booking your flight or drawing up your itinerary and daily plan and using all the tips you discovered in this book to your own delight.

Printed in Great Britain
by Amazon

36219060R00025